ALL AROUND THE WORLD
FINLAND

by Kristine Spanier, MLIS

ogo

T0014707

Ideas for Parents and Teachers

Pogo Books let children practice reading informational text while introducing them to nonfiction features such as headings, labels, sidebars, maps, and diagrams, as well as a table of contents, glossary, and index.

Carefully leveled text with a strong photo match offers early fluent readers the support they need to succeed.

Before Reading

- "Walk" through the book and point out the various nonfiction features. Ask the student what purpose each feature serves.
- Look at the glossary together. Read and discuss the words.

Read the Book

- Have the child read the book independently.
- Invite him or her to list questions that arise from reading.

After Reading

- Discuss the child's questions. Talk about how he or she might find answers to those questions.
- Prompt the child to think more. Ask: Forests are plentiful in Finland. What natural resources are available where you live?

Pogo Books are published by Jump!
5357 Penn Avenue South
Minneapolis, MN 55419
www.jumplibrary.com

Copyright © 2022 Jump!
International copyright reserved in all countries. No part of this book may be reproduced in any form without written permission from the publisher.

Library of Congress Cataloging-in-Publication Data

Names: Spanier, Kristine, author.
Title: Finland / by Kristine Spanier.
Description: Minneapolis, MN: Jump!, Inc., 2022.
Series: All around the world
Includes index. | Audience: Ages 7-10
Identifiers: LCCN 2020050881 (print)
LCCN 2020050882 (ebook)
ISBN 9781636900186 (hardcover)
ISBN 9781636900001 (paperback)
ISBN 9781636900018 (ebook)
Subjects: LCSH: Finland—Juvenile literature.
Classification: LCC DL1012 .S73 2022 (print)
LCC DL1012 (ebook) | DDC 948.97—dc23
LC record available at https://lccn.loc.gov/2020050881
LC ebook record available at https://lccn.loc.gov/2020050882

Editor: Jenna Gleisner
Designer: Molly Ballanger

Photo Credits: Oleksiy Mark/Shutterstock, cover; Shutterstock, 1; Pixfiction/Shutterstock, 3; Alex Stemmer/Shutterstock, 4; Lana Kray/Shutterstock, 5; Erik Mandre/Shutterstock, 6-7; pawel.gaul/iStock, 8-9; Natalia Golubnycha/Shutterstock, 10; Alex Marakhovets/Shutterstock, 11; ullstein bild/Getty, 12-13; ARCTIC IMAGES/Alamy, 14-15; Mariusz Prusaczyk/Dreamstime, 16-17; donatas1205/Shutterstock, 18 (left); Konjushenko Vladimir/Shutterstock, 18 (right); Tanhu/Shutterstock, 19; Henna Siekkinen/Alamy, 20-21; RomanR/Shutterstock, 23.

Printed in the United States of America at Corporate Graphics in North Mankato, Minnesota.

TABLE OF CONTENTS

CHAPTER 1

FAR NORTH

Would you like to go on a sleigh ride? What about a swim in Lake Saimaa? This is the biggest lake in Finland! Welcome!

Lake Saimaa

This country is in Europe. The northern part is in the Arctic Circle. It is cold most of the year. Temperatures can dip to −22 degrees Fahrenheit (−30 degrees Celsius). Brr! Finns warm up in **saunas**.

sauna

Finland has more forest than any other country in Europe. Brown bears, elk, and wolves roam the forest.

Timber is a **natural resource**. It is used to make paper and furniture.

The people here vote for a president. The president chooses a prime minister. This person is the head of the government. Lawmakers meet in Helsinki. This is the **capital**. The Helsinki Cathedral towers above the city.

DID YOU KNOW?

Sweden once controlled Finland. So did Russia. Both fought for control for more than 700 years. Finland became **independent** in 1917.

Helsinki
Cathedral

CHAPTER 2

LIFE IN FINLAND

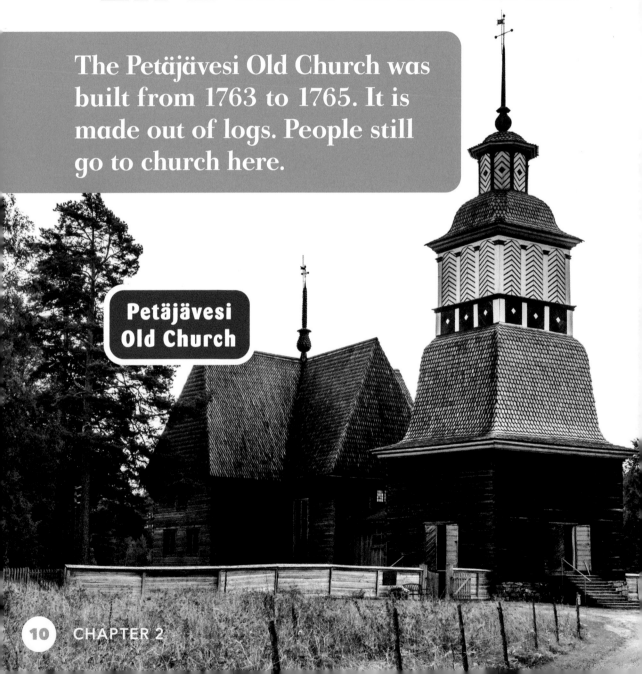

The Petäjävesi Old Church was built from 1763 to 1765. It is made out of logs. People still go to church here.

Petäjävesi Old Church

Glass workers came to Nuutajärvi in 1793. Why? There is forest nearby. They burned wood from it. Heat is needed to melt glass. **Glassblowing** is still popular here today.

glass

Kids here begin school by age seven. They learn Finnish, Swedish, and English. They attend until they are at least 16. Then they have a choice. They can go to high school. Or they can learn a **trade**. College here is free!

DID YOU KNOW?

Finnish kids don't have to wear shoes at school. They take them off when entering their homes, too.

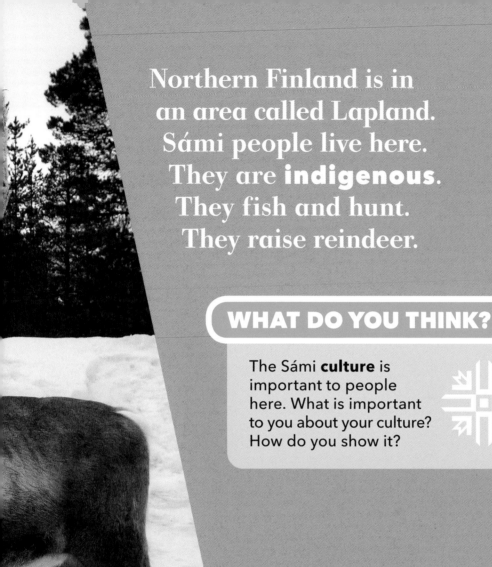

Northern Finland is in an area called Lapland. Sámi people live here. They are **indigenous**. They fish and hunt. They raise reindeer.

WHAT DO YOU THINK?

The Sámi **culture** is important to people here. What is important to you about your culture? How do you show it?

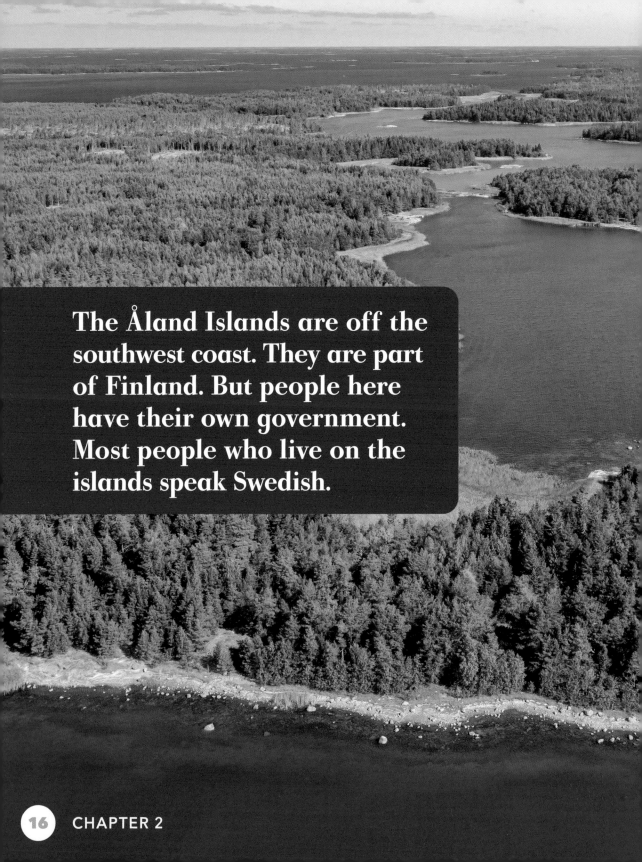

The Åland Islands are off the southwest coast. They are part of Finland. But people here have their own government. Most people who live on the islands speak Swedish.

TAKE A LOOK!

The Åland Islands have their own flag. How is it similar to Finland's flag? How is it different?

ÅLAND ISLANDS FLAG

FINLAND FLAG

CHAPTER 3

FOOD AND FUN

Finland has nearly 209,000 miles (336,353 kilometers) of **shoreline**. That means there is a lot of fishing! Pickled herring is popular. People eat crayfish in summer. It is called rapu.

pickled herring

rapu

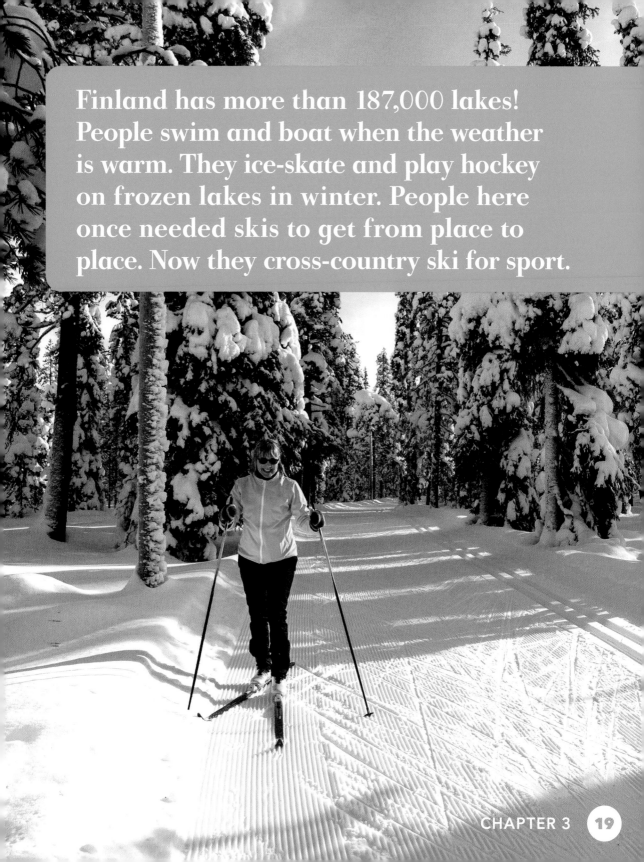

Finland has more than 187,000 lakes! People swim and boat when the weather is warm. They ice-skate and play hockey on frozen lakes in winter. People here once needed skis to get from place to place. Now they cross-country ski for sport.

Juhannus is a summer **festival**. It is a time to celebrate warm weather. People gather around bonfires with family and friends. They dance together. They share favorite foods.

Finland is fun! Would you like to visit?

WHAT DO YOU THINK?

Some nights are never completely dark in Finland. Why? The sun does not set. This is known as the midnight sun. Would you like this? Why or why not?

bonfire · · · · ▶

AT A GLANCE

FINLAND

Location: northern Europe

Size: 130,558 square miles (338,143 square kilometers)

Population: 5,571,665 (July 2020 estimate)

Capital: Helsinki

Type of Government: parliamentary republic

Languages: Finnish, Swedish, Russian, Estonian, Sámi languages, English

Exports: electrical and optical equipment, machinery, paper and pulp

Currency: euro